THE LIFE HE REMEMBERS BEGAN IN COSTA RICA

THE LIFE HE REMEMBERS BEGAN IN COSTA RICA

A Collection of Found Poems

SAVANNAH STONER

FLOATING LEAF PRESS

Published in the United States of America by

FLOATING LEAF PRESS
A division of
WordPlay
Maureen Ryan Griffin
6420 A-1 Rea Road, Suite 218, Charlotte, NC 28277
Email: info@wordplaynow.com
www.wordplaynow.com

Library of Congress Control Number:
2019946397

ISBN 978-1-950499-03-8

For my dad,
who so often reminds me
that things will work out.

I love you.

∞

Contents

Part 1

I was born in Bridgeton, New Jersey, in 1931

and then we moved to Emporia, Virginia, I believe,
when I was about five years old.
I don't remember anything, of course,
about Bridgeton, New Jersey.

We lived in Emporia until . . .
I think it was 1941 or '42.
I'll need to check some of these dates maybe.

But we moved to Costa Rica in 1941,
I think it was,
and for whatever reason
I do not remember anything
from my life in Emporia,
and it's always bothered me.

I've talked to a number of people about it
because I can remember, for example,
your mom
and Angelyn*
and other people talking about—

I think that's when I first realized
that I didn't remember my early childhood

because I'd hear them talking about
their first grade teacher,
and I didn't remember the school,
let alone the teacher.
So there's a big blank
that most people remember that I don't.

I've been reading some things on the computer
about early childhood memories,
and one of the things I have come across
is that immigrant children,
children who've moved
to a completely different culture—
it's not unusual for them
to forget their early childhood.

That makes sense to me.

But my sister, Virginia—
I used to talk to Virginia about it,
and Virginia didn't think it was unusual at all
for people to remember their first grade teacher
and things about their early childhood
if they stayed in the same area
and talked to their friends about everything.
They would be remembering things.

When I finally went back to Costa Rica
and talked to my friends down there,
they talked about things that I had forgotten,
things about our childhood in Costa Rica
that they talked about all the time.

Did it help jar your memory?

Well, about Costa Rica.

I thought that was sort of enlightening
because, see, they talked about things
that happened when we were growing up
among themselves,
but I didn't have anybody to talk to about them.

*Right. So they were able to keep
the memories alive with each other.*

And when they told me about these things,
I would remember some of them.
Some of them I never did remember.

*Author's note: Angelyn was my father's first cousin.

That's the Childhood I Remember

Sandy* and I went back
to Emporia last year
for the 4th of July celebration.

And going back to Emporia, for example,
I went and saw the old school,
and once I saw it—
as a matter of fact when I saw it,
I rode by it
and realized that that was my old school,
or at least I thought it was.
Then I went back
and looked at it better.

Everything looked smaller.
You know how you remember things being bigger?
The school looked small,
but it was my old school.

Anyway, that's been sort of a—
I don't know,
sort of a—
something that's kind of bugged me a little bit
that I can't remember those early childhood years.

But we moved to Costa Rica,
and that's the childhood I remember.

It's almost as if that's the start of—
the life that I remember started in Costa Rica.

And unless I focus on it,
I remember—
I seem to think of myself
as being much younger than I was in Costa Rica.

Obviously, if I was born in 1931,
I think I was nine years old
when we moved to Costa Rica,
which is . . .

> *Well, that's funny*
> *because I've always thought*
> *you were five or six years old*
> *when you moved down there.*

That's odd
because I think of myself as being really small,
but I wasn't.

I was—
they put me in the . . .

That's something else I don't remember.
I don't remember my schooling in Emporia.

And I wish now I had talked to Mother
and gotten some of these dates and ages
straightened out in my mind,
but I didn't.

As best I can remember,
when we moved to Costa Rica,
my parents, Mom and Dad,
put me in the public school,
the Spanish-speaking public school,
and, of course, I didn't understand a word
of anything that was going on.

I believe that they put me in the second grade
in the Spanish-speaking school.
That was when I met my best friend down there,
Mario. Mario.
And, of course, we've been friends ever since.

I don't know exactly why
they put me back in the second grade,
because I think I would have been
entering the third grade up here,
so I'm not really sure of that.

Anyway, I spent one year
in the public school in Spanish,
primarily to learn Spanish,
and that's the first school experience
that I remember.

>   *What was it like when you moved there?*
>   *Did you like it?*
>   *Did you think it was—was it fun?*
>   *Was it scary?*

It was fun. It was—
I mean, school was kind of—
I think it was different,
really different,
but I have good memories of school.

There were some children
that used to pick on me a lot,
and I know that bothered me.

But all in all, the people—
the kids were really friendly,
and I remember them being . . .

At the time there were not many Americans
living in Costa Rica.

As a matter of fact, in that whole school—
it was a big school,
and in the whole school
there was only one other English-speaking person.
You've heard me talk about him,
my friend Charles.
He lives in Raleigh now.

When things would really get necessary,
they'd go get Charles,
and he'd come and translate for me,
so I knew he was there,
and that was a big help.

They didn't want to put me in the same classroom,
I learned later, with Charles.

I learned later that that was because
the best way to learn Spanish
is not to have somebody there
you can rely on.

*Author's note: Sandy is my stepmother. She and my
father married in 1980.

That Kind of School

I went to public school for one year
and then went to a private
English-speaking school the following year,
as best I can recall.

And it was a really small
non-graded school.
The teacher had,
oh, I don't know . . .

I'm thinking back.

She probably had students in there
all the way from the first grade
to the sixth grade
maybe.

She used a correspondence method.
Everybody was on his or her own level.

It was that kind of school.

Lincoln School

The next school I went to was larger.
By that time there were
a few more Americans living there,
and in high school—

I don't remember exactly
what grade I was in
when I transferred to the Lincoln School,
but I went halfway through the twelfth grade
in the Lincoln School,
which was an English-speaking private school.

And the people who went there—
there were some Americans,
but they were mostly Costa Ricans
and children from other countries,
who anticipated the possibility
of coming to the United States to college.

It was a good experience,
a nice, an interesting experience.

There were Costa Rican children,
a few Americans,

and then, for example, I distinctly remember
in the eleventh grade there was a girl
whose father was an exile from Ecuador.

There was another girl
whose father was there
with the embassy from Venezuela, I think,
so there were several South American students.

And it was just sort of a . . .

Like I said, I don't remember exactly
what grade I was in when I moved there,
but I do remember going to high school
in the Lincoln School.

My parents were a little bit concerned.

They wanted me to come to college
in the United States,
and they were a little bit concerned
about how well prepared we were
for college up here.

It Turned Out to Be a Useless Concern

I went halfway through the twelfth grade
in Costa Rica,
and I've never quite known
whether they used it as an excuse
or whether that was really the major reason
they sent me up here,
but they sent me up here
to the twelfth grade in Campbell College,
and their reasoning was that if I went there
sort of as a prep school to go to college,
they'd be sure I was ready.

The fact of the matter is
that I was much better prepared
than any twelfth-grader at Campbell College.

When I was in the twelfth grade in Costa Rica
for that half a year,
there weren't but three of us
that were classified as seniors.
Twelfth-grade Algebra class—three students.

We finished the twelfth-grade book
and started in the freshman college book.

Then they took me out
and sent me up here
and started me over in the twelfth grade again,
when I had already finished that
back in Costa Rica.

At the time Campbell College
was two years of high school
and two years of college.

It was a boarding school.

That was an interesting experience
from a lot of angles
because Campbell College,
to begin with,
was a church school—
still is—
run by the Baptist church.

And so I moved from a Catholic country—
it was really, really a shock,
moving from Costa Rica to Buies Creek.

Have you ever been to Buies Creek?

I don't think so.

Well, at the time—
it's still somewhat that way,
and I don't mean any disrespect to Buies Creek,
but it was out in the middle of nowhere.

I can remember
Virginia and Robert* took me to Campbell College.
We left Raleigh,
and the closer we got to Buies Creek,
I mean, I thought, My God,
where did my parents send me?

I thought they'd put me in jail.

When I was in the twelfth grade in Costa Rica,
we had a civil war,
and a lot of my friends were involved in the uprising,
and I know my parents were worried
about me getting involved,
so in my mind
I thought they sent me up here to school
to get me away from my crowd.

But the funny part about it was—
and I used to laugh about it
because the funny part about it was
that at Campbell College—

if you stop and think about it—
even now,
think about a two-year high school boarding school
out in the middle of nowhere.

Who is going to go there?
You know what I'm saying?

They just had one twelfth-grade class, I think.
They might have had more than that.

But the students in high school
at Campbell College fell into one of two categories:
They either lived right there
somewhere around Buies Creek
and people could afford to send them there,
or they were kids who had gotten in trouble at home
and their parents had sent them there.

You know how they send them.

Not necessarily all of them,
but a lot of them
would be in the same category of students
that would, say, go to boarding school today.

Now, some of them—

Campbell was considered
a prep school for Wake Forest
because Wake Forest is a Baptist school, too,
so some people saw it
as a prep school for Wake Forest
if you felt like you needed prepping
to go to Wake Forest.

But that was my first experience
in school up here
was Campbell College.

It was not a very pleasant experience.
I mean, I didn't like it.

So you were there for one year?

One year—nine months.

And after that, where did you go?

I went back to Costa Rica.
I didn't want to come back to the United States,
so I stayed out of school a year
and came to Wake Forest a year later.

What did you do in that year
when you didn't go to school?

I worked for Dad,
kind of anything and everything,
whatever.

That was at the Coca-Cola plant?

Yeah.

So he was a—
what was his job there?
He was a manager there?

Yeah.

And I really—
you've heard me talk about this before.
When I first moved to the United States,
I felt like a foreigner in a—
and I was
because I'd grown up in Costa Rica
and things were so different.

San José at the time was what I would call—
it was a beautiful city,

somewhere over 100,000 people,
and it was a very cosmopolitan city
because it was the capital of the country
and all the embassies were there,
and so it was definitely a city life
as opposed to Buies Creek
that was out in the middle of nowhere.

So you lived in San José, in the city?

Yeah.

And I did not care for—
I didn't like being out there in the boondocks.
It was very confining.

Very few college kids back in those days had cars.
I did meet a couple of friends who lived in Raleigh,
and they'd invite me to go home with them
once in a while.

But it was just—
it was another cultural shock
if you want to know the truth because—

I don't know whether it is still true or not,
but it was a very, very conservative Baptist school.

They wouldn't allow dancing on the campus,
had chapel every morning.

And that's—
see, I was brought up in a Catholic country,
and most of the time when I went to church,
I went to the Catholic church.
Truth of the matter is
I went because my friends were going
and that's where the girls went.
We'd go to 12 o'clock Mass with Mario.

But I found it interesting
because Costa Rica was
a very conservative Catholic country,
and many of the conservative Catholics
didn't feel like the Protestants were real Christians,
and then I got up here to Buies Creek,
and they didn't think Catholics were Christians.

So . . . weird.

*Author's note: Robert is my father's brother-in-law.

A Pipefitter's Helper

So then after you left Buies Creek
and went back to Costa Rica for a year
and worked with your dad . . .

After that, you—
what happened?
You came back up here?

Came back up here
and went to Wake Forest for a year.

I went back on summer vacation,
then came back up here
for my second year at Wake Forest,
and I went one semester,
and I just quit,
dropped out.

I went to work
for Uncle Bryan in Harrells,
and I never have really—

Looking back on it, you know . . .

When you get older,
when you get mature,
you look back on things
and wonder how things came about.

Uncle Bryan asked me what I was planning to do,
and he offered me a job.

And I didn't—
I was sort of ashamed.

I didn't want to go back to Costa Rica
because I was quitting college
and I was ashamed of that,
and I really didn't know what I was going to do.

When I stop and think about it now,
I think about how crazy it was
to do what I did.

But Uncle Bryan offered me a job,
and I've often wondered since then if . . .

It turns out that back in the Depression, in the '30s,
when things were so bad in the economy up here,
Dad had a good job in New Jersey
with the Coca-Cola company.

Uncle Bryan at the time was unmarried,
but he couldn't find a job anywhere,
so my dad hired him,
and he stayed with them in New Jersey.

And so I wondered later . . .

Putting it all together
after I became mature
and thinking back on it,
I wondered if my dad
had some communication with Bryan
and asked him to give me a job,
or whether Uncle Bryan just did it,
or whether he was kind of paying Dad back
because here I was
up here in the United States
with no plan.

So when Uncle Bryan asked me
what I was going to do,
I told him I didn't really know,
and he asked me if I wanted a job,
and I told him I did, so . . .

He worked for a plumbing and heating company,
and they were building a hospital in Lumberton,

and so I was a plumber's—
a pipefitter's helper in Lumberton.

You may remember Roger.
He was the plumber I worked with.

On weekends I would come home with Roger
and stay at Uncle Bryan's.
We stayed in Lumberton all week.

> *So Roger was the plumber,*
> *and you were his assistant.*

Yeah, I was his assistant.

Uncle Bryan said that—
and I heard it other places, too—
Roger was sudden death on assistants
because he was hard to get along with
and nobody could please him,
but Roger and I got along.

We hit it off great.
It was partly my personality,
but I was determined
I was going to do things
the way he wanted them done.

So I forget now exactly how many—
those kinds of things are kind of vague in my mind—
how many months I worked for Roger,
but it was less than a year.

Home to Costa Rica

My dad called—
or wrote me a letter.

He didn't call,
because there weren't any telephones
in Harrells then.

But he wrote me a letter
and wanted to know if I would come home
to Costa Rica
and work with him,
help him,
and so I did.

And, I don't know,
I worked for Dad for . . .
I'm guessing maybe a year
or a year and a half,
and then—
that was during the Korean War,
and they drafted me.

When I came up to the United States,
I registered with the draft board,

and I got drafted into the army,
and then never went back to Costa Rica until
about ten years ago when I went back for a visit.

So you were drafted down there
and had to come up here
to boot camp?

Yeah.

Where was that? Was that in New Jersey?

Yeah.

How long did that boot camp last?

Boot camp was sixteen weeks,
but I stayed in the army for two years.

It's a long side story,
and I've probably talked to you about it before,
but I was up here in the army,
and the only reason I was here was because—
the only reason I came was because when I—
I registered for—

Robert told me I had to register for the draft.

Robert was in the Marine Corps,
and he was gung-ho about the Marine Corps.

But anyway,
he told me that I needed to register for the draft
when I came up to school,
which I did.

And as long as you were in college,
they didn't draft you.

But then I wanted to go back to Costa Rica.

When I decided I wanted to go back to Costa Rica,
he told me—Robert told me
that I had to get permission
from the draft board,
and I didn't think that much of it,
so I went and got permission
from the draft board,
and they said that I could go,
but I had to promise that if I were called up,
I would come back.

Never dawned on me
that I would get called.

But I did.

I still felt like a foreigner,
so I can remember
being in Costa Rica
and when I got drafted,
my friends said, "Well, you're not going?
Are you? That's not your war.
You don't have anything to do with that war."

So my dad—
I can remember my dad being very adamant about it.
He did not want me to go,
and this caused a—
it was a big to-do in our family.
When I say "our family," I'm talking about
between Mother and Dad
and me
because Dad didn't want me to go.
He wanted me to change my citizenship,
and he wanted me to keep dual citizenship.

A lot of people have asked me since then—
well, not a lot, but several people have asked me,
"Why in the world did you go?"

And the truth of the matter is that I—

what I did—
of course, you have to realize now,
that at that age—

How old were you then?

I was 21, I guess.

But at that age and at that time,
different people lived by different codes.
And I know you've heard people talking about,
you know, the Mafia has one code,
and teenagers have another code.
The code that I was brought up with was
if you said you would do something,
you did it.

And I said—
and what it boiled down to was—
the final—
the last argument that I had with my dad over it—
it really wasn't an argument,
but he was persistent.

I told him—I said, "You know, I signed a paper
saying that I would go back if I were called."

And I said, "I can't—I just can't go back—
you know, I can't go back on my word."

And he—
he—
he tried to tell me that I could,
that I really had no business going over there,
fighting in that war.

But I told my dad—
I said, "Well, if you had signed the promise
to come back, you would go back."

And so he didn't argue anymore,
but he didn't like it either.

> *Did he agree with you that he would go back?*

Well, he didn't say,
but I knew he would.

> *That's just what—because that's what
> he had brought you up with.*

Yeah. That's just the way it was.

And then your mom and I got married

when I had about,
I think, maybe six months left in the army.

And it was not long at all—
maybe two or three months before my time was up,
Mother and Dad moved back to the United States.

They were looking around,
deciding where they were going to live
and what they were going to do.

And that's when Dad met Marvin,*
and Marvin got him interested in growing turkeys,
and that's when he rented the old Kerr place,
where Sam† and Angelyn lived.
Dad rented that.

Well, he called me.
I was in New Jersey, still in the army,
and he called me and wanted to know
what I was planning to do,
and I really didn't have any definite plans.
I had thought probably I would go back to college
on the GI Bill.

But, of course, originally my plan was—
I thought I'd be going back to Costa Rica
because I didn't know they'd be coming up here.

So Dad called me and wanted to know
if I would be interested in moving to Harrells
and going into the turkey business with him.

Of course, I didn't know anything
about the turkey business
except that I knew
that Uncle Bryan and Uncle A.A. were in it,
and your mom's dad was in the turkey business,
and she knew a lot about the turkey business.

And anyway, I told him—
she and—we talked it over,
and I know your mom didn't want
to move back to Harrells, but we did.

We were up in New Jersey,
and that was—
I'm sure you've heard her say
that the last thing she expected—
when we got married,
the last thing she expected to be doing
was growing turkeys in Harrells.

*You know, I don't remember her
ever saying that.*

No? I'm surprised.

*She might have said it,
and I might have forgotten,
but I don't remember Mom saying that.*

Well, it might have just kind of gone
in one ear and out the other one,
but it was no secret, really.
I mean, she wasn't ugly about it,
but she didn't . . .

It wasn't her ideal.

No.

*Author's note: Marvin was a dear friend of my
father's uncle Bryan and uncle A.A.

†Author's note: Sam and Angelyn (my father's first
cousin) were married.

We moved down there to the Kerr place

to go into the business with Dad,
and then, lo and behold,
he died about two months in.
I mean, in no time he died from a heart attack,
and so that . . .

We already had the turkeys in.
I mean, we were in it,
so I decided—
well, it wasn't decided really.
It just was the way things . . .
we had to finish them out.

When the turkeys that we had ordered
were ready for market,
Uncle A.A. asked me—
I was undecided about what I was going to do,
whether to—
but anyway, Uncle A.A. asked me
if I wanted to work with him.

He had always had this idea
of starting a pedigreed breeding farm,
but a pedigreed breeding program is—

well, it's an involved thing,
and it's not something
that he could just go out and hire somebody.
He needed somebody with some sense
and dedicated to it.

So I decided I would do that.

We were living in the Kerr place in Harrells,
working,
getting that pedigreed breeding program underway.

He had big plans for it,
and he wanted to know if I would agree
for Sam and Angelyn to come in
on the business venture.

Of course, I did.

So they moved down,
and for a while we lived in the first floor—
I'm sure you've heard people talk about it.
We lived on the first floor of the Kerr house,
and Sam and Angelyn lived upstairs.

And that really didn't work out.
I mean, that business just didn't—

well, Uncle A.A. died,
that first year.

So Dad died,
and Uncle A.A. died,
and so Sam and I were debating what to do.

In the meantime Uncle Bryan asked me
if I wanted to come and work for him,
and I told him that I did,
that I would.

And so I worked for Bryan for several years.

But the turkey business—
he was in the turkey and chicken business
in a big way.

The bottom line is
it got to the point where
we were working seven days a week
from early in the morning until dark,
and the bigger the turkey business got,
the harder you worked
and the less money you made.

So I decided I wanted out of it,

and that's when I decided to quit
and go back to school.

We had built a little house up on the hill.
And then pretty much you know, I guess,
the rest of it.

I went up to Chapel Hill and talked to them,
and they told me that they would enroll me,
but the man there who was advising me said,
"You've been out of school for so long,
I would suggest you find a small college
to go to for a semester or two
and get back in the swing of things."

As it turns out, it was really good advice
because I wound up going to UNC-W
for two quarters.
I think it was two quarters,
maybe three quarters.
Bottom line is
I took care of all of the required subjects at UNC-W
before I transferred to Chapel Hill,
so by the time I transferred to Chapel Hill—

See, I was majoring in Spanish,
and by the time I went to Chapel Hill,

I'd gotten all the required math and history
and all that kind of stuff.

The only thing they screwed up on was—
you've heard me tell this story, too, I'm sure,
but when I went up to Chapel Hill,
and I thought I had all of my math courses off,
my advisor looked and said,
"Well, you haven't had Trigonometry."

I told him—I said, "I don't want Trigonometry."

And he said, "Well, at Chapel Hill
you have to have it."

Analytical Trigonometry.

That was really disappointing because
I thought I got all my math courses off at UNC-W.

At the time it was Wilmington College.
It wasn't UNC-Wilmington.

Apparently, Wilmington College had
a good relationship with Chapel Hill
because when I transferred—

I mean, there was no problem at all transferring,
except that one thing.

But what was interesting was
my guidance counselor talking about
a smaller college before I tackled Chapel Hill,
I found Chapel Hill easier than UNC-Wilmington.
It was Wilmington College at the time.
That was a tough little college, I'll tell you.

*So at that point
you were going back to school . . .
How old was I when you were doing that?*

You were born—I think you were born
the year I graduated from Chapel Hill.

*So you had Worth and Grace.**

Yeah.

That must have been hard.

Yeah.

*Were you working, too?
Or just going to school?*

Well . . .

How did you do that?

We had—
when I say "we,"
I'm talking about—
your mom and I had chickens.

You may remember the chicken houses
out behind the house.

I borrowed some money,
and we raised chickens.

We hired a man who looked after them
with your mom's help during the week,
and on the weekends—

see, I had to stay up in Chapel Hill,
and I would come home on the weekends
and work with the chickens on the weekends.

It was tough,
but it wasn't bad.
When you're young, you can do things.

Plus, we kept thinking
this will make our lives better.

*Author's note: Here, Worth and Grace refer to my
brother and sister.

In the Back of My Mind

I got my undergraduate degree in Spanish
and started working on a master's degree in Spanish
because my intention was, hopefully,
to teach Spanish at Wilmington College.

Wilmington College was growing,
and the Spanish department was growing,
and so that was in the back of my mind.

That was my thought.

It may sound egotistical, but at the time
Spanish teachers were in short supply,
in huge demand.

Chapel Hill was considered
one of the three top language departments
in the whole country—top three or top ten.
Anyway, it was way up there.

And when I graduated in Spanish,
the year I graduated from Chapel Hill in Spanish,
there were only three of us
that graduated in Spanish from Chapel Hill.

Wow!

And I got offers
from all over the United States to teach.

You did?

Yeah.

Just from the undergrad degree?

That was with—yeah.
I had a teaching degree in Spanish.

And so when I say I had hopes of getting on at—
if I said that today,
it would sound kind of stupid, I think,
you know, that I planned to get on at UNC-W
in the Spanish department.

I don't think it sounds stupid.

But at the time it was not—
it wasn't all that farfetched.
I mean, I was bilingual, and . . .

Had lived in Costa Rica . . .

Yeah. And Spanish teachers were in high demand. I think I would have stood a good chance.

I was teaching Spanish

at Sunset Junior High School,
and the assistant principal retired—
resigned. He wanted to do something else.

And the principal asked me
if I would be assistant principal.

I had to think about it really hard
because I—
that really had not even—
I hadn't even considered that.

I mean, until he made that offer,
I was planning to be a Spanish teacher.

So at first I told him
I wasn't interested.

And he said, "Well, think about it
and try it for one year."
He had his reasons for wanting me to take it.

And so anyway, I finally told him that I would—
that I'd try it.

And it meant more money,
a little more money than teaching.

But once I got into it . . .

You liked it?

I didn't dislike it.
Yeah. I think I—you could say I liked it as a job.

Of course, it was odd
because for at least one summer
I went back to school to keep
working on my Spanish,
master's in Spanish.

Then the superintendent offered me a job
as a principal.

Of course, I didn't have a principal's certificate,
but in those days—

I don't know whether it's still true or not,
and even if it's true,
it probably wouldn't happen much,
but in those days,
you could work on a provisional certificate.

They paid you just as much,
but if you didn't have a principal's certificate,
you could work as a principal,
provided you were working toward your master's.
So that's what I did.

Where did you get your master's degree from?

Chapel Hill.

And where were you living at that point?

In Harrells.

So you were living in Harrells,
working as a principal in Wilmington,
and getting your master's degree
in Chapel Hill?

Yeah.

Dad, how did you do that?
Holy cow! Oh, my God!

My friend Art and I used to drive to Chapel Hill
every Saturday to take classes,
and I took summer classes.

I finally finished the master's.
Finally got it.

It got old.

I drove—
I commuted from Harrells here to work for, I think,
seven years.

> *Seven years.*
> *So did you guys have the chicken thing*
> *still going at that point,*
> *or . . .*

Yeah.

> *Is that why y'all stayed in Harrells?*

Yeah. Partly.

I don't remember exactly
when we gave up the chickens,
but, yeah, we had the chickens
even after I was working down here.

I don't remember exactly when,
but not too long after

we quit that though,
we moved down here.

Part 2

What other questions have you got?

Well, when you were a boy,
what were some of your favorite things to do,
like, with Mario?

Did you have sports that you liked?

Or were there—
I remember that picture of you
playing baseball or softball.

We played pickup games
of baseball, and, of course, in Costa Rica
soccer was the big sport.

So you played that?

Well, I played.
When I say "I played,"
I don't mean an organized school team
or anything like that,
but that's what we played
during recess and after school.

And on Saturdays Mario and I would go out to—

there was an athletic field
that we would go to sometimes
and play pickup—
there were always a lot of people out there,
and they'd get two teams together
and play pickup baseball.

And Mario and I played tennis quite a bit.

A Horse Apiece

And then at a certain—
I don't remember exactly how old I was,
but my dad bought Doug* and me a horse.
Two horses.
A horse apiece.
And one of the things I remember
a lot about doing a lot of
was horseback riding.

I loved horseback riding.

Trails and up in the mountains,
and we lived—
well, for a while we had the horses outside of town,
and then Dad built a house outside of town
in a little place called Escazu.
Of course, when we lived out there,
we had the horses right there near the house.

And, gosh, on weekends,
I rode every—
all day almost every weekend.
We had several different horses.
And that was one of my favorite things to do.

Doug and I were talking about it
the last time he was down here.

Sometimes we would—
Mom would pack us a little lunch, you know,
and he and I would take off
up in the mountains on the horses
and stay gone almost all day.

*Author's note: Doug is my father's brother.

Doug

*Were you and Uncle Doug close
when you were growing up?*

I wouldn't say that we were close.
Probably—
partly because of the age difference, I think.

What is the age difference between you guys?

Well, let's see.
I'm, I think, three years older.
And, of course, now that's—
three years' difference in our ages . . .

Once you get a little bit older,
that's no difference at all,
but when you are sixteen
and your little brother is thirteen,
there is a big difference.

So we went through an age where,
when we were doing all that horseback riding,
the pre-teenage or early teenage years,
where we were pretty close.

But later . . .
and I guess this is sort of a natural thing
because of the age difference . . .
we weren't close.
We didn't do a lot of things together.

I think one thing that factors in is when—
once one brother gets a driver's license,
that has a tendency to—
you're just older.

Your interests are different.

Virginia

Virginia was, I think—
gosh, Sandy would know.
She knows everybody's birthday.

I think Virginia was seven years older than me.
But she . . . let's see.
When we moved to Costa Rica, she—

I think she only went to school down there
for one year
and then came up here to college.
Back in those days,
if I'm not badly mistaken—

Virginia didn't go to the twelfth grade.
She may have,
but I think they would accept you in college up here
if you'd been through the eleventh grade.
I'm not sure about that.

Anyway, I do remember that at that time,
she was the youngest student
ever enrolled in Meredith College.

And I can remember Virginia coming home—
by "home," I mean to Costa Rica during the summer.
I remember particularly one summer she came home
and brought a friend with her,
and I can't remember whether she came again or not.

It's funny how you remember certain things.

One thing I remember about Virginia
coming home that summer was
she wanted to ride my horse.

At that time I think we had four horses,
and I told Virginia that she'd be better off
riding another horse.

Virginia, I think, thought
I just didn't want her to ride my horse.
That wasn't it.
He was not easy to handle.

Anyway, I told her—I said,
"Well, you know, you haven't ridden very much,"
and I said, "He's not a—
he's not . . .
easy to get along with."

And—
but she wouldn't—
she wanted—
she made up her mind.
She wanted to ride that one.

So anyway, they left,
she and her friend.
She had a friend with her named Valerie,
and they left.

You may have heard this story before.

About 30 minutes later,
I saw them coming down the road.

Virginia was walking,
leading.
Valerie was riding her horse,
but Virginia was leading my horse,
walking.

She was really upset.
"He won't do what I want him to do."

I told her—
I said, "Well—"

I was irritated
because the last thing you want to do
is let the horse get the best of you
because I knew—

I said, "Well—"
and I told her—
I said, "Well, you should have never led him home.
He'll never let you ride him again."

And she said, "I'm not planning to ride him again."

His name was Cholo

Cholo?

Cholo.

What does that mean?

It means—Cholo is a black.
He was black.
Cholo means a really dark black.

It's—I don't know how to explain it.

It's kind of a—what—
we have a word in English for a really dark black.
Is it ebony?

Ebony? Um-hum. That's black.

That's a real black,
but you would never name a horse Ebony,
I don't think.

But this one—
Cholo was another word for black.

What was Uncle Doug's horse's name?

His horse—
well, that was the second horse I had.

Doug had a horse named Lucky,
and I had a horse named Black Diamond.
Those were the first two horses that we got.

Cholo came along later.

At one point we had four horses
because Mom and Dad liked to ride.

And when Mom would ride,
she would ride,
always ride Lucky.
He was a really nice horse and really, really tame,
easy to get along with.

He's Not Easy to Ride

When I went back to Costa Rica
and saw different friends,
I ran into this one girl—
woman, and she said,
"The biggest thing I remember about you
was you rode by my house one day
on a black horse,
and you stopped,
and we were talking,
and my next door neighbor—"

I knew what she was going to tell me
because it scared the pure hell out of me,
but I knew what she was going to say.

Her next door neighbor wanted to know,
"Oh, can I ride him? Can I ride him?"

I was on my way to take him
to get new shoes put on him.

And anyway, I knew better,
but I told her—
I said, "Do you know how to ride?"

And she said, "Oh, yeah, I've ridden a lot of horses,"
or something like that.

I knew—
I told her—
I said—
I told her the same thing I told Virginia, I think,
"He's not easy to ride."

But she said, "Oh, I'll be fine.
I've ridden lots of horses."

So I said, "Well, okay."

She ran into her house
to put some jeans on
and came back out,
and when she got on him . . .

We were in town.
This was in town,
and they lived on this hill,
and the street didn't have intersections
along where they lived.

I'll never forget it.

There was this wall,
and then this street that went down next to this wall,
but it went down and into a boulevard
where there were just lots of cars,
and the streetcar went up and down that boulevard,
and there was a lot of traffic.

Well, anyway, she got on him
and was doing fine until,
I don't know,
something scared him or something happened,
and he started to run down the hill,
and she couldn't stop him,
and there he was running on asphalt and . . .

But this is what this girl—
this woman was telling me,
"What I remember about you is
you chasing after that horse,
trying to catch him,
going down the hill."

Somehow, by some miracle,
when they got closer to the boulevard,
that horse realized that there was traffic,
so he started to brake,
but he was on that asphalt,

and he would slide,
and I could just see both of them just—
it scared me so bad. It scares me now.

> *But she was able to stop him,*
> *and she didn't fall off?*

She didn't stop him.
He stopped.
And I led him back up the hill.

> *I'll bet she was scared to death.*

She was.
She wasn't as scared as I was though.

Bragging

I loved horseback riding,
and I was really good at it.

I mean, I used to brag that if it had four legs,
I could ride it.

Of course, I learned differently,
but I used to—
you know, you get hooked on something.
I was just hooked on horseback riding.

And it was a perfect place to ride horses,
lots of dirt trails and dirt roads,
and ride up in the mountains.

It was a just a . . .

It was just a great—
a great life.

What We Ate

What do you remember about the food
in Costa Rica?

I don't remember that much about it,
because at home we ate American-style food.
I gradually got used to eating Costa Rican food.
One of the things I still like is black beans and rice,
and that was the national dish in Costa Rica.

But one thing about it as far as food is concerned
that I do remember—
well, several things, but—
you had to be really careful about what you ate
because of—oh, what's the name of it?
Amoebic dysentery.

And so we followed a strict rule:
If you can't cook it or peel it,
you don't eat it.

Another thing you had to be really careful about
was the water.
We had to boil all our water that we drank.

These days, we would have bought bottled water,
but back in those days,
there was no such thing as bottled water.

So we boiled—when I say "we,"
Mother boiled all the water that we drank.

But there's something else
I remember about Costa Rica:
My dad would go to the market
and buy a whole bunch of bananas
and hang them up on our patio,
and as they would ripen,
we would eat them.
We never were able to eat them all.

And they were so cheap.
Now, you have to realize
we're talking about a long time ago,
but if I'm not mistaken, in those days,
you could buy a whole bunch of bananas
for the equivalent of 10 cents in the United States.

Wow!

When Mario and I would get out of school,
there were these people

selling popsicles and things.
And there was this one man
who was always out there.
He had a cart full of small pineapples,
and he had this machete,
and so you could buy a pineapple,
and he would peel it,
and then you would hold it by the—
what do you call it?

The stem?

Yeah, the stem.
And eat the whole pineapple.
They were so good,
and they only cost about,
oh, a nickel maybe
for a whole pineapple.

Wow!

Now, by contrast there were no apples.
All the apples were brought in from the United States
and were extremely expensive.

But you probably had . . .
what did you have, papayas?

Had papayas. In our backyard
at one time I can remember
we had trees that grew
lemons, oranges, bananas, avocados.

I got so sick on avocados one time.

We had a lot of fruit trees
in our backyard.

What Mother Did

Well, as far as doing things,
she liked to substitute
in the English-speaking school,
so she did that.

And she did some tutoring,
teaching people how to speak English.

And then—I hate to admit it,
but the truth of the matter is
that I don't really know.

Of course, when I say "I hate to admit it,"
I don't know whether you would remember
what your mom did
when you were that age.

I don't. I don't remember.

I just—
I know I remember
seeing women over there
at our house, visiting.

And I do remember her going to school to teach.
She liked that.

And—
but really, I don't really know what she did.

When we first went down there,
she had two maids,
a fulltime housekeeper and a cook.
And she would tell the cook—
tell them what she wanted cooked.

When she first moved down there,
I'm sure a lot of her time was spent
trying to learn how to speak Spanish.

But later on in life, later . . .

I don't really know what she did
up until the time when
Dad built that house out in the country.
It was outside of town.

Then he bought some lots
and built several houses for rent,
and Mother would go out there
and supervise building the houses.

Oh, wow!

And I remember she bought one—
or he bought one that they remodeled
and made it more modern.
It was a very typical Costa Rican
stucco house,
and they remodeled it
and made it a really nice looking house.

I remember that.
She spent a lot of time doing that.

But Mother never,
never learned how to drive,
which I never understood.

And, of course, she would not have wanted
to drive in San José anyway,
I don't think.

But, you know, she never drove
even when they moved back to the States.

*I always wondered about that
because I know that she didn't.*

But I didn't know if she'd had a bad experience
or something or . . .

I just don't know,
because I know I mentioned it to her several times.

I told her I'd teach her how to drive,
but she wasn't interested.
It really limited what she could do up here.

Our Long-Distance Friendship

Do you still keep in touch with Mario?

Very, very seldom.
Of course, I saw a lot of him when I went down there,
and I had thought we would keep closer touch,
but we really haven't.

Rio Blanco

Didn't you take a canoe trip?
I'm trying to remember the details.
Tell me that story.

My friend Charles and I rented a dugout canoe,
and he and I were talking about it not too long ago,
as a matter of fact,
because I can't—

I can't imagine our parents letting us do what we did.
I mean, it's mind-boggling, really.

But we—
his father was the general manager
of the railroad that led from San José
down to the Atlantic Coast.

And when we were in the—
it may have been the year
that I was in the twelfth grade.
He was a year behind me.

But anyway, to make a long story short,
it was when we were either

in the eleventh or twelfth grade,
and we had a few days off.

His father arranged—
they had one of these put-put cars, as it were,
up and down the railroad,
little old cars, you know,
but they'd run on the railroad tracks.
And he arranged to have one of those
take us up an old line
that wasn't used anymore
and drop us off.

And it—
I want to say it was a week,
but it wasn't a week,
it was probably more like four days,
but he dropped us off
with the understanding that in four days
he'd come back and meet us there.

Here we were, two teenagers.
We had rifles with us.
We were going hunting.

When we got to the end of the line
and he dropped us off, we—

I don't know how far we walked,
but we walked a ways,
and we rented this dugout canoe from this guy.
It was his canoe.
But when I say a "dugout canoe,"
I'm talking about the real thing.

Dug out.

Dug out of the log.

Charles was the planner in the thing.
He had it on his mind
that we wanted to go somewhere
where nobody had ever been before.

And so he had heard about this river
called the White River,
Rio Blanco,
which means White River.

And we were going to paddle up to that river
and go up the White River
as far as we could go.

We went—
this is a funny story.

We went up the White River,
and, as a matter of fact,
we even chopped—
it was not a very big river,
but at one point
we had to clear some stuff to get through,
so we could go on up the river.

The reason they called it the White River was
because you could see the bottom
like you can at White Lake,
see all the way to the bottom.

Anyway, we went up the White River
and pitched camp.
We didn't go all the way,
but we pitched camp.
That's where the monkeys drove us crazy.

Our idea was that we would paddle up the river.
It wasn't a really fast-moving river,
so we'd paddle up the river
as far as we could
and then early in the morning
we would get in the canoe
and let it drift down the river.

You could see these trails where animals
would come down to the water,
and Charles's idea was
we would be ready and shoot—
we would see something coming down to get water
and kill 'em.

But the monkeys followed us in the trees,
"Yack, yack, yack, yack,"
and threw things
and just . . .

      As you were drifting down?

Yeah. They scared everything away,
so the only thing we ever saw was monkeys.

But the funniest part of the story was
that we paddled way up Rio Blanco one day,
and we got out.

We saw this place
where it looked like a trail came down to the water,
and we thought it was an animal trail,
and so we decided that we would tie the canoe up
and go up that trail
and see if we could catch something.

We walked up that trail,
and all of the sudden
we walked up to this clearing,
and there was a little thatch roof house
out in the clearing,
and there was a family living there.

And, I mean, it was a typical old jungle house
like you'd see on television,
had a thatched roof,
adobe walls about that thick,
no windows,
just open,
doors open.

And, oh, they were so glad to see us.
They couldn't believe it.

So it turns out, they lived there,
and they would just go to town,
I don't know,
once in a blue moon and buy supplies.

But the funny part about it was
that they asked us if we wanted some coffee,
and we didn't want to insult them,
but at the same time

things didn't look very sanitary.
I don't know if we wanted coffee or not,
but we finally told them,
"Yeah, that would be nice."

We went inside and sat down at this table
on these homemade little benches,
cross benches, like that.

We were sitting at the table,
pretending to sip at the coffee
when this pig came through one door
and ran under the table
and knocked my bench over
and ran out the other side.

He was oinking hard,
"Oink, oink, oink."

But in these areas like that,
that's the way people lived:
doors were wide open,
animals lived right there,
chickens were walking around loose in the yard.

It was just really cool.

So a whole family was living out there?

Yeah.

I forget now.
I remember there was a man and a woman
and, I don't know, several children.
I don't remember how many.

They were really decent—
you know, they were really nice people.
They were really odd people
to be living way out there.

And he was telling us about how
he killed stuff to eat.
They had a garden,
and he told us how often they went into town,
but I forget.

They had to go in the canoe—
I mean, he would go.
He said he would go in the canoe.

And it was kind of a pitiful, pitiful life,
but that was an interesting trip.

I think about it now.
You know, as a parent
it would never have occurred to me
to agree to a trip like that for any of you all,
because . . .

Charles and I were thinking about it, too.
That guy dropped us off
and if something had happened to one of us,
there was no way we could have gotten out.
I mean, if something serious had happened to us . . .

> *Right. They wouldn't have known*
> *how to find you.*

Plus, I think probably if they had come for us
in four days
and we weren't there,
they would have tried to find us,
but they didn't know we went up Rio Blanco or—
there was nobody to ask.

We didn't see—
that was the only soul we saw.

But the main thing is it just—
I've thought about it a lot.

If one of us had gotten injured,
I don't know what we would have done.
I really don't.

Almost Ancient History

Doug and I spent a lot of time talking
the last time he was down here,
and we have trouble after so many years
with the scope and sequence
of exactly when certain things happened.

We both said we were going to start
writing experiences down
because, like, you're interested,
and when you stop and think about it—
we were talking about this, too—
by the time—well, look at little Worth,* for example,
by the time he is in his 30s or 40s,
the things that happened to us
will be ancient history almost
and would probably be interesting to him.

It's like now
I wish I had taken some time
and really talked to Grandmother,
or even Mother,
but especially Grandmother,
to see how things—
what things were like.

Yeah. So much has changed since then—

Oh, yeah.

—in the world.

Unbelievable.

*Author's note: Here, Worth refers to my nephew.

Special Thanks

To my husband, Andy, for being my love, for cooking all our delicious meals, and for nudging me to "Go write!" Thank you for giving the manuscript a good read. You're my guy.

To Maureen Ryan Griffin, my teacher, mentor, and friend, for your steadfast support, for editing the manuscript with a loving and light touch, and for shepherding this book into the world. I'm so thankful.

To Jen Walls, for painting the beautiful black horse for the cover. You're amazing! Thank you, thank you, thank you! To see more of Jen's enchanting artwork, please visit her website, www.jenwalls.com.

To all the members of our Thursday night's Under Construction class, Amy Brinkley, Michael A. Clark, Elizabeth Delaney, Justin Hunt, Seth Langson, Barbara Linney, Charles Murray, and Linda Whitesitt, for your enthusiasm, kindness, and wonderful feedback. I'm so grateful to be on this journey with you.

To Ellyssia Rogers, for our many years of creative camaraderie. You have been a huge support to me throughout the process of writing this book. Bless you!

And to Isabella Rupp, for your generous spirit and unwavering friendship, for always encouraging me to stretch creatively, and for reviewing the manuscript and sharing your insights with me. You're the dearest, sweetest, most inspiring friend I could ever hope for.

And most of all, to my father, Jack Maynard, for sharing your life's stories with me, for reading an early version of this book, and for giving its publication your blessing. These poems simply wouldn't exist without you. I'm so proud to be your daughter.

DEC • 64 •

About the Author

Savannah Stoner lives with her husband, Andy, and their two dogs in Charlotte, North Carolina, where she is writing her first novel.